memories from an irish village school

& other tales

by

liam ó caiside

ISBN (Paperback): 978-1-5272-7694-9

ISBN (E-book): 978-2-5272-7693-2

Editing by Dustin Bilyk @ The Author's Hand

Front Cover Design by Aoife Cassidy

Printed by Ingram Spark in the United Kingdom.

First printing edition 2020

For those children who went to school with fear in their hearts and a knot in their stomach.

contents

FOREWORD

I grew up on the side of a wooded hill about a mile from a tiny village of no more than 200 people. Surrounded by hard-working hill farmers, almost everybody was poor, but we were sustained by humour, great neighbourliness, and music.

Most houses had a fiddle on the wall, which was an invitation to anyone to come over, take it down and play. A week in our house would rarely go by without some kind of revelry. If a farmer sold a cow, saved the harvest, or got the turf home, these were all good reasons for a session. Gossip also played a big part in our community, usually featuring the same old characters regularly complaining about each other. This was usually done in good fun without any nastiness.

My father was a professional soldier and away a lot. Our mother bore eight of us at home, supported by the community nurse, who lived in a neighbouring town six miles away and would arrive on her bicycle. She didn't always make it on time, but with the help of neighbours we were all delivered safely.

My siblings and I often marvel about how our mother coped. With little in the way of amenities we take for granted today, she always managed to turn us out clean and neat, and home was always warm and cheerful. She was a great optimist and would often say in later years that she never knew what depression was.

She was outspoken when she felt something needed to be said. In those days, it was rare to challenge the local establishment. Rarer still for a woman to do so. But I remember her speaking out many times when she felt there was an injustice or someone was being treated badly.

Mother was also the go-to person in our neighbourhood. Neighbours would be regularly dropping in and would always be offered tea and her homemade bread. She would be sent for when babies were being born, called upon when a dead body needed to be prepared and laid out, and the first person ready to help when dinners needed to be prepared for farmers when the corn was being thrashed. She was never hassled and took everything in her stride.

As for me, I had an idyllic childhood. That was until I reached Room 2 in our local school. Room 1 was great.

Here we had a kind, middle-aged teacher with a large family of her own, and she treated all children well regardless of their backgrounds.

Master was the complete opposite. We had to endure him from 3rd class and upwards for four years until we moved on to secondary school or into the workplace. He was a vindictive, bigoted, and cruel man who beat, berated, and humiliated the kids he took a disliking to, and all the more to those he considered underprivileged.

My experience of what he did to us has been seared in my memory for six decades. The memories have been running around in my mind for all that time and only growing with intensity as I age. I believe that the stories, and the children they are centred on, deserve to be told.

I have also included a couple of amusing tales of a fascinating and eccentric family of neighbours who were a joy to be around. I have often thought that if our great novelist and playwright, John B Keane, had lived in that neighbourhood, he would have immortalised them. They were some of the finest, wittiest, and most delightful people I have ever met.

Finally, I recount some fond memories of a great friend who was an endless dreamer, optimist and romantic.

Through these stories, hopefully readers will get a glimpse into the past of a small rural community that was in no way unique. Similar communities and experiences existed all over Ireland. Some children went to school excited and uplifted by wonderful teachers, and others went like I did—with a sick feeling and pain in my stomach.

It is also my hope that you will be uplifted by my positive memories of great neighbours who, through their humour and wit, brightened our community on dark days, and of a dear friend who dared to dream.

the exam

I started primary school the same day as Anthony. I remember him as a bright young boy who loved playing football, fishing and doing all the usual stuff that kids got up to. He got along well with our teacher, who was a kind middle-aged lady with a large family of her own. She always tried hard to make every child comfortable and give them the best start in life.

Anthony was in the leading group of kids in class. She would regularly praise him for his work, and it seemed that he was destined to cruise through school, as he was comfortable with every subject. He loved going to school in those early years and was as happy on Mondays as he was on Fridays.

But that changed when we completed second class and moved next door to Master's room, where we would remain for third class and upwards. He was a tyrannical teacher, unpredictable in his moods, and he beat pupils he took a disliking to mercilessly. When Master wasn't beating them, he would berate and humiliate them in front of the class, and this was particularly so if they came from underprivileged backgrounds.

This didn't happen every day. Some days he would come to class in a good mood, particularly if something nice had happened for him like catching a large salmon in the river or lake. But the moment he walked into the classroom we knew from his expression what kind of day it was going to be. Would it be a day that could be enjoyed or tolerated? Or was I going to spend my entire day praying that I wasn't going to be picked on?

Those few who came from what were considered well off backgrounds had no such worries. They came to school each day and, regardless of the quality of their work, would escape unscathed.

The incident which changed things for Anthony happened in fourth class. He had escaped the wrath of Master up until then and was still comfortably among the top performers in all subjects. But one afternoon, Master was in a vile mood. A girl was standing at the blackboard, and Master was screaming at her to solve a math problem. She had long, thick red hair and he was pulling it and shaking her. She was so scared she was unable to speak.

He called up Anthony to show her, but he was also frightened, and he froze and was unable to function.

This was something you didn't do in Master's class. He shouted at Anthony, practically foaming at the mouth with rage. The more he shouted the more frightened Anthony became, and when he didn't immediately solve the problem, Master hit him with all his force on the side of the head.

Anthony's head bounced off the blackboard and he fell to the ground. I am unsure if he was knocked unconscious or if he fainted, but the teacher next door heard this and came in. She slowly helped Anthony to his feet, took him outside, gave him a drink of water, and sent him home. Master was still shouting like a madman, but we could also see he was a bit worried. He turned to the other teacher and said, "I hit him because he was stupid!"

To her credit, as she was leaving, she responded, "He wasn't stupid when he left me."

After this incident, Anthony ceased to learn math. As a kid I did not understand what was going on, but he just stopped learning. Looking back, I think he froze when the subject was being taught. He continued to excel in other subjects but relied on copying from fellow pupils for math.

He went to extraordinary lengths to hide his problem from Master. He would duck to the toilet when he sensed that he may be about to be asked a question. He even considered burning the school down at one stage so he could escape, but then he remembered that he had overheard the teachers discussing maintenance that was required on the school and that they had planned to relocate to the town hall for a period while that would be carried out.

There was a constant strain on Anthony. He came to school each day with fear in his gut. Fridays became a blessing and were anxiously awaited, as were holidays. On those days, the pain abated for a bit but would re-emerge on Sunday, growing in intensity as the day went on. He would go to bed with his pain and wake up with it. The fear of being found out as a cheater in math became an obsession with him.

He made a point of sitting beside Kevin, who was good at maths, but not at Irish, so they copied off each other in a handshake agreement. But as time went on, Kevin realised Anthony needed him more than he needed Anthony, so he began to subtly increase the pressure. He would delay showing him his work, making him even more nervous. On the rare occasions Anthony had sweets, a substantial share would be demanded by Kevin. It just got worse from there.

We would have football games at lunchtimes. Kevin would ask Anthony to play in goal and to let in an easy one or two to allow his team to win. To my knowledge, Anthony never allowed that to happen, but to his lasting shame he pretended to go along with it. Once, when he was invited to join a group of boys planning on doing Christmas Mummers, Kevin, who was not included, declared that if Anthony participated there would be no more copying allowed. Anthony defied him and sweated for two weeks until Kevin needed help with an Irish essay. Soon, cooperation resumed, but the threat of losing his copying partner was always at the front of Anthony's mind.

He used to fret constantly about the exam he would have to take at the end of his final year. What was he to do? He prayed fervently in church, at bedtimes, and everywhere else, looking for a solution from somewhere. For some reason, it never occurred to him to ask his classmates or anyone else for help, likely because he thought he was just stupid with numbers and no amount of help would work.

About halfway through the final year, out of the blue, Master took ill and a young, female teacher was drafted in to replace him. It was her first teaching job. She was single, pretty and caused a bit of a stir with the young men around the village.

Anthony took this as a sign from heaven. Maybe his prayers were answered, and she had been sent to help solve his problem?

But his hopes were soon dashed. On her very first day, seating arrangements were changed, and Anthony found himself sitting beside someone who was a class lower and unable to help him in any way. On the same day, she set out a test on the key subjects. As usual, Anthony sailed through everything easily but presented pretty much a blank page for math. When collecting them she looked at him with disdain, got red in the face with anger, and told him he was stupid and that he would fail the exam.

What angers me to this day is that it did not occur to her to question why he could top the class in all other subjects but fail badly on math, and from that day until the last day of class, she ignored him. Even when he put his hand up to answer a question, she ignored him. Never once did she acknowledge his existence or offer any kind of help. To Anthony this was almost as bad as being beaten. Every day he felt belittled. Every day he blamed his own stupidity for it.

Of course, her predictions were correct. Anthony topped the exam in all subjects and failed math. He felt humiliated but tried hard to hide it. In those days, therapists only existed in movies, so he bottled up his feelings and tried to move on.

On the day the results were out, he went to the village to shop for his mother and was looked upon with pity by the locals. The news was out all over the village that he was the only one to fail. Such news is big news in a tiny village.

Anthony went on to secondary school for a couple of years but dropped out before taking any exams of note. He then went off to the army and served abroad a couple of times. He learned a lot in the army, including the fact that he could learn math after all. After the army he went to London where he joined a large manufacturing company. Before he was twenty-one, he had been promoted to Supervisor, responsible for about forty people. Soon, he was sent to college by his employer where he excelled in all subjects, including maths. There he learned that education was a joy, rather than something to endure, and afterwards, his career continued to progress, and he became a senior operations manager. He later went on to manage factories and supply chains around the world for a global company and built a reputation for being one of the very best in that world.

He later founded his own consultancy business. His services are still in demand all over the world. He has won international awards, has had papers published, and is a sought-after speaker at conferences worldwide. And yet, despite his worldly success, the pain he felt going to school all those years ago, the crippling fear of being found out as a cheater, still returns to him regularly. To this day, he still feels the hurt, and the anger that came later, of how he was mistreated by Master and then humiliated and ignored by a young teacher fresh from training college who should have been idealistic and anxious to help all of her pupils. He often wondered what motivated her to do that.

Finally, one day many years later, Anthony wrote to her. He asked her what made her treat a twelve-year-old boy like that. Was it the environment in which she was raised? Or was it what she was taught in teacher training college?

She replied that she could not remember, but if she hurt him, she was sorry. She said she would like to meet him.

He replied that she had not answered his questions, and that he saw no advantage for him in meeting with her. He added that he bore her no ill will, but that he wanted her to know about the hurt that she had caused.

Things changed in school environments very quickly after we finished our education. Free education was introduced in the famous O'Malley bill in 1967. Parents would no longer accept that their children would be routinely beaten, and new generations of teachers took the fear out of the classroom.

On occasions when Anthony would be visiting home, he would see the kids going to and from school and marvel at the laughter and joy that they exuded. He would wonder at the transformation from his years of fear and mourned that he was not born a few years later.

Overall, he has had a successful life. He has a loving and supportive wife and three beautiful daughters. He has been successful with work and business. He has been active in sports all his life and is healthy and fulfilled. However, the memories he carries from childhood and the climate of fear in the little two-roomed village school all those years ago still return to haunt him. He has accepted that they will until the end of his days.

He still talks a lot about those times. When we meet, we are quickly back there reliving it. We remember many things, but we especially remember the children that were treated worst of all. Those who were beaten and humiliated most regularly…they are all dead. Those were just from our generation. Master taught there for several decades.

It will never be known the numbers of children he damaged and how many died prematurely because of it. It haunts me to think about it, and so I will end this story here, leaving it in the past where it belongs.

the traveller boy

David was about nine or ten years old when he and his younger sister, Sarah, came to our school. They were settled travellers and had moved recently to a small, run-down cottage about a mile from the village. I cannot recall where they came from, but I think it was somewhere in the east of the county.

Master had a jaundiced view of anyone from a deprived background. The poorer the background, the worse he treated them, and coming from a travelling background only added to that. He had a special contempt for David and his sister.

There were no fat kids in those days, but David and Sarah were thinner and paler than the rest. I heard adults say they were malnourished, but their mother had done her best and cared for them the best she could. Their father was in and out of prison for stealing, and with little social security support in those days, it was difficult for her to hold things together. However, they turned up in class clean and as well dressed as most other kids. They were shy, well mannered, and most surprising of all, they performed well in their classes.

Soon after they arrived, it became known that their mother would occasionally take a drink and could be aggressive. We all found out because an elderly woman, notorious for being a gossip, used to sit in her front room at night with the lights off and listen to what was going on at the street corner. Everyone in the village knew about their situation because the old woman didn't hold back when she spread gossip about the mother.

Apparently having had enough, one night the mother threw a stone through the old woman's window shattering the glass all around her. She was arrested, spent the night in the barrack cell and was later taken to court and fined. Truth be told, there were plenty of locals who delighted in the old gossip getting a bit of medicine. Given the chance, I think many villagers would have done the same.

David and Sarah's mother would visit our house from time to time. Like everyone who came to our door, Mother made her welcome. She would give her tea, homemade bread or cake, and send her off with a bag of something that would be useful at home.

Once, I overheard her telling Mother that the landlord, a local farmer, would call for the rent, but when she did not have the money, he would take it in another way. I remember she was crying and upset when telling this, but I didn't understand the implications at the time. However, as I grew up and understood her situation, I could only admire her sacrifice to keep a roof over her children's heads. It is to my mother's great credit that she did not condemn her. Rather, she offered her sympathy and understanding.

One day, we came to school to discover that the black baby boxes, that all schools had in those days, had been stolen. Every month, each child was expected to donate a penny, and the proceeds were then to be donated to religious orders who were caring for children in Africa.

The local guard was sent for. They found footprints and the markings of corduroy pants on the window where the thief entered. We all knew David wore similar pants and boots, and he was also absent from school the day the box went missing. Master informed the guard that he and the boy's father were suspects. The dad was arrested, and it turned out that he had used David to get the black baby box, for he was slender and small and could easily enter through the window of our school. From what Master told us, they stole from a couple more boxes in other parishes as well.

Both father and son were charged and brought to court. The father received a prison sentence, but instead of extending sympathy to a son misled by his father, the Master wrote a letter to the judge saying how poorly disciplined David was, and how he was a bad example to the rest of the school. He recommended he be sent to an industrial school.

We all knew this was untrue. David was well disciplined and caused no problems for anyone, but Master was so vindictive towards anyone from such a background and he was determined that he be sent away. He took the trouble to attend court so he could read the letter to the judge himself. His vindictiveness was rewarded. Despite his mother getting on her knees and begging the judge not to send him away, her words fell on deaf ears and David was sent to Letterfrack—a notorious industrial school in Galway from where horror stories of how kids were physically and sexually abused emerged years later.

I recall his mother crying bitter tears when relaying this story to my mother. She was as heartbroken as any mother could be. I don't recall seeing Sarah in school ever again.

Every so often, Master would read the letter aloud to the classroom, boasting and taking credit for putting David away. What he didn't realize was that David wasn't a bad example to us. Even at our age we could discern what had happened. It was always our impression that he was a decent young lad, who would not have done such a thing without being made to do so by his dad.

I saw David a couple of times when he returned on holidays. He had filled out a bit and said he was ok with being at the school, though he never elaborated much. We went fishing a few times and we were both delighted one time when he caught a large trout. It was 3.5lbs and one of the largest caught on the local river for years. James, the local shopkeeper, took a photo, wrote a short report, and ensured it would appear in the Derry Journal. It was a generous act to a young lad who had experienced little enough of it. His mother was particularly pleased and proud, and brought the article to my mother to read.

I cannot recall how long they were living in our neighbourhood, but a few years later, I was walking down a street in Dublin city and saw him jump out of a car and enter a shop. He would have been sixteen or seventeen then. I waited outside and he emerged with packets of sweets and biscuits. He was with several other young men and said he was going to a job. We only had a moment or two and I have never seen or heard anything of him since.

Growing older, one appreciates the impact of childhood events on our lives. How we were treated by parents, school and society are forever seared in our memories. David and his sister would not have good memories. One wonders how they coped with life and if they found some of the happiness that eluded them in childhood.

the ambush

There were days when Master was calm and would philosophise about things. He would speak to us like we were adults. But mostly he was boasting about his beliefs, his friends, and his hobbies.

Sometimes he would talk about politics and football, but most often, he spoke about religion. He was typical of the village snobs that were looked up to and feared in that era. Each community had its own self-appointed elite that ruled the small towns and villages. You crossed them at your peril.

More than any other subject, Master would speak with disdain about the lifestyles of those who were poorest and the conditions in which they lived. He did not mention names, but we all knew who he was referring to in the small village.

Apart from being vain, arrogant, and a bully, he was also a religious bigot. He would pontificate about Roman

Catholicism being the one true religion. To him all others were fake, and its followers were doomed to damnation.

It's important to note that, in those days, Ireland was not multicultural like it is today. In 2020, you will find several nationalities and different beliefs in every town and village, never mind our cities which are cosmopolitan just like London or New York.

But back then, other nationalities were mainly in the cities. There were some Indians who ran textile factories and had the odd restaurant. There was also a smattering of English and Scottish scattered here and there. Where we grew up in Donegal, we had quite a few English gentry and first-generation Scots whose parents had grown up there. With religion it was about 80% Catholic and 20% Protestant, but all this was before the troubles that erupted in the late 60s, and, at the time, relations were exceptionally good between the two communities. It should be said that they also remained that way right through the struggles in Northern Ireland.

Declan was a bright, energetic young lad, one of the tops in our class. He was also a natural leader, and after one of Master's rants on religion he decided to do something for the Roman Catholic cause. He told us boys he was arranging an attack on some of the Protestant kids as they travelled home from school.

He had an uncle who had served in WWII and had found some book belonging to him on how to stage ambushes. Choose high ground where possible, with plenty of cover to hide. Make sure you have the element of surprise. "They need to be taught a lesson," he said. "They need to understand that we are the one true faith." He put out the word that he needed volunteers. "Not wimps or sissies," he said. "I need boys prepared to fight."

No doubt about it, Declan was planning this like a military operation.

Being thorough, he put a fair bit of thought into it. First, he recruited only boys who could show that they were keen to participate. Interviews were in the boys' toilets and those considered unsuitable were dismissed out of hand. As I recall, two of the girls also volunteered but they were rejected with derision. In those days, they would have been considered a liability. This activity was very much seen as hardy boys' work.

Although both my brother and I were sorely tempted to participate just for the excitement, we had Protestant neighbours just up the road and we got along great together. Their parents were warm and friendly towards us; we played with their kids regularly and worked on the farm together. Their uncle Billy would even give us a lift in his lorry when he came upon us, so we decided we couldn't live with ourselves if we participated in Declan's military operation.

So, Declan planned his ambush without us. He had already selected his ambush point and had stockpiled some ammunition there. On the big day, lunchtime was spent gathering stones and sods. These would be launched from a high ditch disguised by trees on a road out of the village that several of the Protestant kids would be taking. Some bows and arrows were also to be deployed. In anticipation of the victims then being in shock and disarray, the plan was to charge them with sharpened sticks fashioned like spears.

Laden with guilt, but without all the details, my brother and I went home on that fateful evening and told our mother about it. She thanked God that we had the sense not to take part and said that no good would come of it. We all had to respect our neighbours regardless of class, colour, or creed—a lesson she would repeat many times as we grew up, and something that stood us in good stead when we went off into the wide world.

The ambush went ahead as planned, and the schoolyard was full of tales of it the next morning. Everything did not quite go to plan though. Stones, sods and arrows were launched, but when the charge came, instead of retreating, the Protestant boys stood and fought. By all recollections, they give a good account of themselves, outnumbered as they were. These were big, strong, strapping boys hardened by farm work. As for the Roman Catholic boys, a few of them carried the marks of battle. They seemed proud of their wounds and were showing them off, especially to the girls.

Later that day, our local Garda called and asked Master to step outside. Clearly some of the parents had reported the event and he had come to investigate. They were outside about twenty minutes or so and we were in suspense, wondering what was going to happen. I knew for sure Declan and his platoon would get battered. The excitement felt by the boys involved in the scuffle was now replaced by fear.

When Master returned, he was pale, but we could also see that he was fearful and looked nervous. He ranted and raved for a while about what an outrageous thing it was to do and how shame was brought upon his school. He said, "Were you not taught that we must be kind and tolerant of those who were of different persuasions?"

No, he had preached the exact opposite, and by the way he treated those he deemed different, we knew he was a hypocrite.

In the end, nobody was beaten. It was a complete climbdown. He knew it. We knew it. And he knew we knew it. For once, just once, we had seen our Master humbled. For the first time in years, all in the world seemed to have fallen into a right place.

I do not recall him ever mentioning our Protestant neighbours after that.

lessons in vindictiveness

My brother called me to say that Brian had died. He had been suffering from cancer for some time and had finally succumbed.

Once again, I thought back to my childhood and the two-room school in our village. I could see Brian as vividly now as I could then. He was a bright, mischievous young lad that came from the junior room where the teacher was kind, patient and understanding. But, like all of us, he eventually ended up in Room Two where hell on earth awaited some.

There Master reigned supreme. It was his fiefdom where he could indulge his prejudices, bigotry, and frustrations on the kids he was charged with by the state to prepare for adulthood and the big world that awaited them. Kids like Brian came to school knowing that if they escaped the day without being bullied, humiliated, beaten and kicked around the classroom, it was a rare and fortunate day.

Room Two had third class and upwards, so this was not something that was going away any time soon. It was a four year stretch and, looking back, few prisoners would have had a tougher sentence. At that age, a week could feel like a lifetime, and our solace was weekends and holidays. For Brian, it was also mitching. For this he would always pay a heavier than usual price when he returned.

Brian came from a difficult and poor background, making him the ripest of targets for Master. He was raised by an elderly loving couple who were unrelated to him and who, for a time, lived close to our house on the side of the hills among small farmers. They were eccentric and considered odd in their ways, but when I think back, they undoubtedly loved each other, as they did Brian. They allowed their fowl and piglets to wander in and out of their kitchen and had a great respect for all things living. This environment made it an enjoyable home and as kids we loved to visit. Later, they bought a larger farm on the other side of the village. We were all sad to see them move, because they were liked and respected by my parents, neighbours and, of course, all the children.

Almost sixty years on, I still remember Brian being battered. When he was not being beaten, he was being verbally abused and humiliated. Little wonder then that, as the years wore on, he came to school increasingly less, for which he was battered more. I recall vividly one particularly bad session when Master roared at him, "You look like a pig, act like a pig, smell like a pig, now you must grunt like a pig!" Master then proceeded to grunt, roaring at Brian to do likewise.

When Confirmation became due, we turned up in our Sunday best, which for many families was also everyday best. Brian was turned out in a nice dark suit, white shirt, red tie, and new black shoes—one of the best dressed from our class. Master was seen entering the sacristy prior to ceremonies commencing, and the word came out that Brian was not to be confirmed.

Later, Master boasted that he was responsible for this, telling the Bishop that this boy had not been coming to school regularly and would be unable to answer religious questions. Even as nine-year olds, myself and many of my classmates felt the injustice of this. I can recall the look of dismay on his elderly guardians, who were simple folk from the mountains, powerless to challenge such a decision.

When his elderly guardians passed away, it was assumed that Brian would continue to live and work on what was considered, locally, a substantial farm. However, being quite innocent in the ways of the world, they had not made any legal arrangements for Brian to do so. Relatives of the guardians stepped in and took over the farm. There was no place for Brian. All right-thinking locals thought that this was wrong and had little doubt that he was meant to inherit it.

Shortly after, Brian, along with one of my brothers and some other lads, emigrated to Birmingham. As they waited for the bus to begin their journey, Master spied them, came over and enquired where they were going. When they told them, he looked at Brian and said, "You will never make it back."

Even in a moment like that, when young men, excited and apprehensive, were leaving their homes and neighbourhoods to try and find their way in the world, Master could not resist twisting the knife.

The following Christmas, Brian *did* come home and spotted master in the local pub. He went over and said, "I am back, Master." It was one rare moment of satisfaction for Brian to which Master had no response.

In Birmingham, he worked hard, did not succumb to heavy drinking like many other young lads, and met a girl from the other side of the county. They got married and she inherited her family farm. They returned to Donegal in the late 1970s, raised a family and ensured they got the education that Brian was denied. I never met him after I moved away, but my brothers would see him occasionally. Considering the hardship he'd endured as a kid, he'd done well for himself, although no one knows what kind of dreams he had when he went to bed at night.

He died quite young, like so many others from that small school that suffered likewise at the hands of the Master. Those that suffered most during my years at that school are all dead. I do not believe that is a coincidence.

The Dreamer

Edward was a handsome young lad with plenty of confidence, dark wavy hair, and a way with girls that most of us envied him for. He was a dreamer with a new ambition every week, and sometimes more often than that.

However, he'd had a complicated upbringing. His mother had died when he and his siblings were small. His sisters and brothers were raised by aunts—strong women who had no fear about voicing their opinions on anything and everything. As for Edward, he remained at home with his father, but he contracted a serious illness and died when Edward was only fourteen.

He was a year ahead of me in school and good in all subjects. He never suffered at the hands of Master because his aunts were both respected and feared. They would not have tolerated any of their family being mistreated, and Master was careful not to upset them.

Edward was full of mischief and one of the leaders around the village as we grew up. He became the head altar boy in our church at an early age, which carried with it a bit of respect. Soon, he became responsible for recruitment and training, as our priest didn't involve himself in those matters.

He convinced me to enlist, and on my very first mass told me just to watch but didn't allocate any of the tasks to me. That was until the priest suddenly announced a "short holy hour" to immediately follow mass.

He had a habit of springing that on the congregation from time to time, and I used to hear a lot of the grownups complain about it, because other parishes would have theirs on an evening. The grumbling was intense, because football matches often took place on Sunday afternoons and, and the holy hour would eat into that time, and although he called it a "short holy hour", it wasn't anything of the sort.

Our neighbor, John, figured that if he had it on an evening, only the same faithful few would turn up. Those precious few were the holiest of the holy who were often seen trying to out pray each other. John figured the priest wanted to assure he had a full house – that he was like a singer that needed a large crowd.

Master was one of those holiest of holies, but his reverence in church sadly didn't match his behavior in the classroom.

So we were lined up and ready to return to the altar to commence the holy hour when Edward suddenly propelled me to the head of the line. He handed me the thurible with the burning incense and told me to keep it swinging during the ceremony. The nerves in my body fired off in warning.

All I knew was that this task required two visits to the priest on the altar during the ceremony, but I didn't know the particular moments these took place. Edward reassured me.

"Don't worry, Liam. I'll cough when you need to make your move."

I wasn't happy about this, but I had no time to argue as the priest had started leading us out. So, about five minutes into the ceremony, Edward coughed, and although I wasn't expecting it that soon I stood up and made my way to the priest. Immediately I knew I'd messed up, bad.

He looked at me and growled, and in a loud whisper he said, "I'm…not…*ready!*"

His whispers were infamous. They could usually be heard 200 yards away in the village square, and so anyone in the church who might have missed my premature humiliating move was made aware of it then.

Dutiful Edward coughed a few times after that, but I had lost confidence in his process, and so I waited until the priest gave me the nod.

Afterwards in the sacristy, an inquiry was launched to find out what had happened. Edward reckoned he had a tickle in his throat and couldn't stop the cough, but I was very doubtful about that. One of my other friends, Johnny, didn't believe him either, and landed a right hook on him just below the eye. He had a black eye for two weeks. The priest heard the scuffle and came in and told us to go out the back and finish it there as he was not going to allow that sort of carryon in his church.

Another time at the church we were at confessions. Usually, as a minimum, we were expected to attend the first Saturday of each month. We would have been thirteen or fourteen by then, and usually confession took no more than a few minutes in total—two in the confessional box and then another one or two to say penance.

The plan was to all head to the football pitch for a game afterwards. Johnny and I were out in the usual time, but Edward seemed to be in longer than usual, which had us all curious. When he came out to say his penance, he was on his knees for what seemed an age. We had no idea what had happened, but he seemed to have been inflicted with a lengthy punishment.

When he finally left the church, he said that the priest had told him he was turning into a right corner boy and that he needed to mend his ways. In those days, "corner boy" was no more than young lads hanging around the village square trying to look clever and whistling at the girls! He had given him three decades as a penance.

We were shocked by such a severe punishment and were still debating it when we reached the football pitch. One of the older teenagers reckoned that such punishment must be right up there with the serious stuff, like premarital sex or even infidelity! It didn't make sense.

However, Edward's reputation was inflicted no harm at all amongst the older lads as some of them suspected he might have been up to some mischief with a girl and was withholding the information from the rest of them. I never did get the straight story from him.

One summer, Courtney's Travelling Show came to town. They were one of those famous fit up troupes that toured Ireland in the 1950s and 60s. They put on short plays, had clowns, comics, and a show band. Versatility was the name of the game and they all had multiple roles. I would guess they had about fifteen or twenty members: a mix of adults, teens, and kids. All had multiple parts to play and they would entrance the village for an entire week once a year.

One of their young ladies, probably about fourteen or fifteen years old, would check the audience in each night then disappear and reappear later in various acts. As I recall, she also played saxophone in the band.

Our Edward fell hopelessly in love with her and announced one evening that he was going to run away with the show. When I made further enquiries, he told us he had based his decision on her asking him to look after the entrance for a few minutes while she ran to the toilet. No other encounter had taken place, other than she had given him a free pass for his stint at the door. However, this was enough to convince Edward that she had chosen him over all the other young lads hanging around. He was sure she liked him for much more than just a short relief at the entrance.

Most of the village, young and old, also feared the aunts. These women, though good-hearted and kind, could shrivel a tree at fifty paces if they took a dislike to it. So, when I enquired how he was going to inform his aunts about his imminent departure, Edward said he had it all figured out.

He produced a letter addressed to them both, stating he was convinced this was his vocation and that he hoped they would understand and support him. He added that, when he returned next year with the show, he would ensure they got free passes each night. He had it all figured out and said he would mail the letter on the day prior to departure. He planned that, by the time they had read it, he would be several hours away.

When I ventured to suggest they may not be pleased with this idea, Edward said, "If they don't like it, they can bugger off, because I'll be thirty miles away by then playing to packed houses and taking my girl for walks on the beach." Apparently, the grand plan was well advanced, and he declared that he had already started to get his things ready.

The next day, we decided to go fishing before the show, and as we wound our way along the river, we spied the girl of his dreams walking hand in hand with an older boy from out the country.

Edward was devastated. Dream shattered. He considered challenging this young lad for her affections, but decided against it as he was older, bigger and a member of the boxing club. We all knew he'd wipe the floor with Edward, but some of us would have loved to see him challenge him for the young lady's affections. Instead, survival instincts kicked in. By the time the show started that night he was already vying for the affections of a Belfast girl who was holidaying with her aunt for the summer.

His father, already quite ill at this point and unable to work, asked me once if I would help Edward win the turf in the nearby bog. My mother warned me not to take any money for this as she said he was ill, had lost his wife, and could do with the money.

So, we spent two days in the bog together. It seemed to me that most of the work fell to me because Edward had ambitions to be a singer at this stage. Among his favourites were the Dubliners, who were making a name for themselves at the time. He regaled me with their version of 'McAlpine's Fusiliers' for two days straight, and by the time we were finished I knew every verse backwards and never wanted to hear the song again!

I met him a few days later, he told me that my payment, that I was forced to refuse, was instead pocketed by Edward himself. He had spent the money right away on trips to the cinema, minerals, ice cream, sweets, cigarettes and one of our favourite treats in those days: fish suppers in the Dolphin Café. I didn't even get an ice cream out of it!

Well it took me a while to get over that I can tell you. There was a fair bit of spending in thirty shillings in those days. Half would have gone to my mother and I still would have had enough to fund ice cream and crisps for a couple of weeks plus a few trips to the cinema.

I thought I would take my revenge on Edward by not thanking his father. However, when I eventually did meet him, he was with one of the aunts. I said nothing for a while as he enquired about my parents and such things. However, as bad as it would have been exposing Edward's deed to his dad, it would've been nothing compared to what the aunt was likely to do to him. Still, I was tempted.

But cooler heads prevailed…or, rather, we had a match coming up on Sunday and we needed him for that. I knew his aunt would inflict a lengthy confinement and would never allow him to travel, so I cracked under the pressure and thanked Edward's father kindly for the money I had not received. In turn, he thanked me for my efforts, but I got a baleful look from the aunt who was probably feeling like my mother did—that payment should not have been accepted!

Years later, I went off to the army and Edward went to study in a local hospital. I would meet him when home on leave and he would get fired up by tales of where I had been and would declare he was also going to join up. But it always seemed there was always another distraction to keep him from doing so.

Once, when on leave after an overseas stint, I met up with him and hitchhiked to a local dance. I was togged out in trendy new gear supported by a nice tan, and Edward always looked good. We had big ambitions that night. Never lacking in confidence, he was hitting the floor with the best-looking girls in the hall even before the band had finished tuning up.

As for me, I had eyed a bunch of fellows arriving from a neighbouring town. They considered themselves hard men and delighted in rising rows. To put it simply, dancing was not high on their agenda. Edward, who was giving it all on the floor, and I, with my tan and trendy gear, were magnets for them, and I could see them shadowing us and waiting to make their move. We were heavily outnumbered and, fit as we were, we could not handle six or seven of them.

I tried to draw Edward's attention to this, but he was oblivious to the threat and only had eyes for the girls. Just when an attack seemed imminent and I was eyeing down a possible escape, Seamus, a fellow from their town who I had gone to secondary school with appeared. He was known as a hard man and a character. He had been expelled from school for a while because he had told our young and attractive English teacher that she had nice bouncy boobs and he would like to see them. She went into shock as did the rest of the class. When she recovered, she hit him two hard slaps across the cheeks and took off for the headmaster.

I cannot recall the sentence Seamus received, but it was severe enough and he was banned from her class for the rest of the year. She would not remove her jacket in class for ages after that, even on the warmest of days. Around the school and town his reputation soared. The boys were seriously impressed.

More important to this moment, I stood with him once when a few of the hard lads from another town were threatening him. I decided it was time to call in that favour, so I made a bee line for Seamus. He was delighted to see me and wanted to hear all about my adventures overseas. It was clear to all those around that we were friends, so the threats abated and both myself and Edward, who remained oblivious, had a narrow escape.

Inevitably, Edward got bored with working at the hospital and, after a couple years, moved to England. Over the years, he worked as a carpenter, bricklayer, firefighter, as well as countless other jobs I cannot recall. He also made quite a name for himself by fronting an Irish band that played the dancehalls and Irish clubs around that area.

Restless as ever, Edward moved back home after a few years, became a successful builder, and continued to make music. I met him once in the 1980s at his uncle's wake, and we had a few drinks and swapped experiences before parting again. He looked well and was as full of dreams as he was when he was just a boy.

A few years ago, I heard that he was terminally ill and in a local hospice. He had sent a message via his niece that he would like to see me. Of course, I visited, and for a couple of hours we were lads again, back in the 1960s, swapping our dreams and tales of what had and might have been.

I said goodbye with a heavy heart, but he was laughing at something I said as I walked out the door and that helped me on my way. A few days later he passed.

We remember many of those we grew up with, but some more than others. Edward I will never forget.

breaking lent

I saw Eddie coming out of the wood and over the rocks. It was getting dark and I assumed that he wanted one of us to go to the village and get his usual items, typically a half pint of Bushmills and a half dozen of Guinness.

On the other hand, the last trip for him was yesterday. Two in all—one for me and one by my brother. Each visit was worth half a crown, and ten and eleven-year olds could do a lot with that. Usually he would be up much earlier when he was on the drink, but he had not appeared all day and I had overheard my mother say that the pensions were gone again, and we would have to wait another month before fighting over who would get the half crowns.

I hoped he was not going to ask us to go and get it on tick. This would happen now and again, but the publican was never happy about it and would complain to us like we were the ones who were responsible. Moreover, if we went before he received his next pension check, there was no half-crown on offer. Sixpence maybe if we were lucky.

However, it was different this time. I could see a worried expression on his face. He asked my mother to come down and see his sister, Maggie, as she had been asleep since midday yesterday and he could not get a budge out of her.

Maggie was a spinster and lived with her brothers Eddie and John James. Like us, they lived in the middle of the wood on the side of a hill about a mile from the village. We lived about a quarter-mile apart. We shared a well in the woods about halfway between us, and any time we were despatched for water, our mother would tell us to bring a bucket to them too.

Maggie was in her sixties and the brothers were in their early seventies. John James had been a well-known IRA figure in the war of independence and been in the first batch of graduates of the Gardai Siochana. Eddie had been a psychiatric nurse and it was said that more pensions came into that house each month than any other for miles around.

More than anything, they all liked a good drink. Eddie and Maggie would consume at home, but John James would save his pensions for a few months and then go on a bender in the village until his money had gone. They ran a small farm and kept a few cows and some fowl. They were very kind to them, and it was said that their animals were better treated than most families around. Each of them had individual names and were usually named after those who lived in the neighbourhood. Some neighbours were not too happy about this and would complain about being named after a duck or a calf.

I also remember that their house was always full of books, magazines, and papers. People would arrive with a bundle and leave with one, a bit like how a library would operate without the administration. However, Maggie had a sharp memory and woe betide those who would take but not bring. People would come from miles around and it was known as a house where everyone was welcome. They had two fiddles on the wall, and it was said that on a good night the revelry could be heard in the next parish!

My mother asked me to get on the bike, go to the shop and ask John to ring the doctor to come and see Maggie. She took off with Eddie down through the woods. I got to the shop and John, who had one of the five phones in the village, rang the doctor who said he would be there in a couple of hours. When I got back to the house, my mother was sitting by the bed holding Maggie by the hand. She said she still had a pulse but not much else, and she could not get a peep out of her. "To kill time and to help her we will say the rosary," she said to me.

A rosary is a tough assignment at any time, but with just three people it's a real challenge. Two are going to end up with two decades each, and I knew that Eddie wouldn't be volunteering for a second one!

Finally, the doctor arrived. He was a genial, elderly man who treated all his patients with respect. Neighbors always said he enjoyed visiting that household because he was usually smiling as he left.

He seemed to be in with Maggie for ages, and I heard Mam telling one of the neighbours that they would need to start thinking about organising a wake. Finally, he came out with a little smile and asked Mother, "Does Maggie take a drink?"

"Of course," Mother replied. "She does, and a good one at that, especially when the pensions are in."

"Well, I have given her something that will bring her around soon. Make her a strong mug of tea and put a lot of sugar in it, will you?"

Mam prepared the tea and brought it into Maggie who was stirring a bit by now. She helped her up in the pillows and she took a sip from the mug. She hesitated for a bit, opened her eyes, and asked if there was sugar in it.

"Well yes there is, and plenty of it."

Maggie give her a cutting glance and replied, "God forgive me…I have broken lent!"

Mam give her a long look that I recognised. It was used rarely and only when she was seriously annoyed. She was no doubt thinking of the dinner that still had to be cooked, the cows that had to be milked, and God knows what else had to be done.

Finally, she replied, "Maggie, you might consider giving something else up next year!"

the mart

When Eddie was visiting, he would usually come on the path from his house through the woods and then over the rocks to where we lived a few hundred yards away. The path could be tricky enough, especially when it was wet or frosty and it was easy to slip and fall.

When he arrived that day, I could see that Eddie had fallen—one of the legs of his trousers was wet and mucky. We could tell he had a couple of drinks in him, because he was always a bit unsteady on his feet when he had. My mother said to him he should stick to the road when he had a drink in him, that he could fall and split himself and that he would be dead before someone would come across him.

He was a great character well known and liked by everyone who knew him. His drinking was legendary, and it was said that if he still had even half of the money he had spent on drink that he would be a multi-millionaire. He had retired recently from a hospital in a neighbouring town and enjoyed a decent pension. He loved music and song and was a decent fiddler until the fifth drink when his fingers would get confused.

He asked my mother if I could go to the mart with him tomorrow morning. This meant an early start, usually just as it was getting bright. Eddie had a heifer he wanted to sell, and debts to settle. The mart was in the next town about seven miles away and the local farmers would walk their animals on the back roads.

I was about twelve at the time. It was a good two and a half hours of a walk with an animal. My job would be to stay up front of the heifer and prevent her from going into fields or down laneways. I had done similar trips with other neighbours and had always been well rewarded for it to the amount of ten shillings, an Ulster Fry in Rodden's tea house, and then a bus ride home. I had once gotten a full pound from one of the other farmers when he sold his heifer at a particularly good price, and I also knew Eddie was generous when he had it. I felt I would get at least the ten shillings if not more, so I was delighted with the opportunity.

The next morning, my mother had me up early and gave me a good breakfast: porridge, boiled eggs, and her homemade bread. I have travelled many parts of the world since then, but never have I found bread to compete with hers. She was famous for it and people from all around would call regularly for a cup of tea and a slice or two.

She told me it could be one or two o'clock before Eddie could take me for tea in town, so she demanded that I eat plenty. She also made a sandwich for the road and told me to put it my pocket as it could come in useful later. Little did I know then how prophetic her words were!

She was a bit worried about Eddie and said he would probably go to the pub after the sale, so she made a special point of telling me to get him to the square for the bus at half four. Eddie had a sister Maggie, and when I called to their house to start the journey, she also told me to keep him away from the pub if at all possible, but if he went to be sure I got him out for the bus.

Maggie was an interesting case herself and loved her animals more than most people. She always got attached to them, and when I went by to pick up Eddie and the heifer, she had tears in her eyes. The heifer was called Sally, and she told me to be gentle with her. I thought to myself that, if Sally behaved, I would absolutely treat her kindly, but if she did not, I had an ash plant that I would not hesitate to use.

The journey in was uneventful enough. We met the odd van or tractor and the occasional man or woman on bikes heading to the town for work. These were small narrow roads and had little traffic. It must have been autumn because the weather was quite cool and the evenings drew in a bit, but after a mile or two, I warmed up and enjoyed the journey. I was thinking I was a real grownup now, looking forward to Rodden's fry and spending the ten shillings. I would bring some treats to be shared at home, go to the cinema a few times, and still have enough for a couple of fish suppers in the Dolphin Café. I would be a real man about town!

We got to the mart about mid-morning, and Eddie got the heifer installed in a pen to be viewed by the buyers. At certain times, each animal would be paraded, and people would bid on them. I overheard the auctioneer say we would have to wait no more than an hour, maybe less. He and Eddie seemed to know each other well, because Eddie said he would buy him a drink in Fox's later if things went well.

I thought this was great. Once the sale was complete, we would go straight to Rodden's for the fry. Eddie would then head to the pub and we would have about two hours before the bus was due. I figured I could wander around and meet up with some of the lads I was at school with.

But then the unexpected happened; something that neither my mother nor Maggie had anticipated or prepared me for.

After Eddie chatted with the auctioneer for a quick moment, he suddenly said to me that he was going to see about something and would be back in twenty minutes. I had a bad feeling about that. I knew he had great difficulty stopping when he had his first drink, especially since he had worked in the local hospital in that town for almost forty years and had drinking friends everywhere. I knew it was bad, but he had sprung it on me, and before I could think of a way to stop him, Eddie was gone.

Half an hour passed, then an hour. The man in charge came by, and when I said Eddie would be back shortly, he looked a bit doubtful. "Let's hope he's not in Fox's bar," he said, "because if he is, it might be a bit longer than that."

He was right. Hours went by. All the while, farmers stopped by anxious to put a bid on Sally, but they got fed up with me saying Eddie would be back in a few minutes, and after a while they stopped coming.

As we got well into the afternoon, things started to wind down. Almost all the cattle were sold, and the place was emptying fast. Farmers were heading home to do the milking and other chores before it got too late.

Sally was getting fed up at this stage too. There were buckets and a water tap, and I gave her plenty, but she was hungry, and I could only find a small bit of hay. I had already devoured mam's sandwich at this stage and was starving. A farmer who was eating biscuits from a packet in his pocket took pity on me and gave me a couple, but I was dreaming of Rodden's Ulster Fry and this was no substitute.

Finally, at about four o'clock, Eddie arrived back. He could barely stand and said he got delayed a bit. 'Some delay,' I thought. 'Four bloody hours!' I was getting desperate at this stage. There would be no Rodden's fry, no bus and we would have to walk Sally back home. To make things even worse, I wouldn't get no ten shillings either because that was dependant on the sale of Sally. And to top it all off, it was going to be dark in an hour or so and I had no idea how I was going to manage the two of them.

Eddie insisted that we had to sell and said that he could not face Maggie if he did not. She had a temper and a wicked tongue, and I had heard from the grownups that when she was in a mood like that, all were to stay far, far away.

Despite Eddie's insistence to sell, the man in charge came over, smiled at Eddie and said, "It will have to wait until next month, Ed. Sales are closed, but we can have that drink you promised me next month, OK?"

"Right," Eddie said, looking at me a bit guiltily. "We'll have to head for home then." He searched his pockets and found a few pennies; all he had left from his afternoon at Fox's. He gave them to me, and I ran to the square and bought a bar of chocolate. I devoured it.

It must have been half four when we set off up the hill, past the cathedral on the long climb out of the town. I kept thinking I should have been on the warm bus, well fed and with money in my pocket. Instead, I was facing the nightmare of getting them both back home and it was getting dark soon.

Eddie was wobbly and would occasionally fall. I had to help him walk, which meant that Sally had no one in front to keep her on the main road. We were barely out of the town when she slipped away through an open gate and into a field. There was plenty of grass there and Eddie told me to let her feed for a bit.

After about ten minutes or so, she seemed happy enough, but in the meantime, Eddie had fallen asleep. He was stretched out in the ditch snoring and it must have taken me fifteen minutes to get him back on his feet. I did consider leaving him there but was fearful he might die of the cold. I also remembered the older folk saying that, years ago, Eddie had threatened a neighbour who had refused to go to the village and get him whiskey, saying that he would come back and haunt him from his grave when he died. The man had since passed away, but they said he hadn't had a day's luck after that moment. I was not going to take that risk I can tell you.

So, we set off again. We were making slow progress and it was dark and I was desperate. Then I had a brilliant thought.

I thought that, if I could get Eddie up on Sally, we might move faster. That if I could get him face down and draped across her, it might just work.

Sally did not take that well at all. She looked at me accusingly as if to say, "This is not my fault!" No way was she allowing that to happen.

Sweating, the both of us now reeking of booze, we finally made it home. It took us almost five hours, and I was beyond exhausted struggling to keep Eddie on his feet.

Thankfully, Sally was well behaved and seemed to know she was on the way home. This time, when the opportunity to enter the many open gates presented itself, she ignored them and continued on her way.

As we got closer to home, Eddie began to sober a bit, though I would venture to guess that it was the thought of facing Maggie's wrath that truly sobered him.

When we finally got to their yard, Maggie was waiting and frantic with worry. She had a set of beads clutched in her hands and said, "I'm on my third rosary, for God's sake! I thought you were in an accident!" If, as expected, we had come on the bus, we would have been back hours ago.

But Maggie's relief quickly turned to anger when she saw the condition Eddie was in and, worse, that there was no sale. Before we left that morning, my mother had said Maggie and Eddie needed the money to pay bills.

As I look back now, one of the remarkable things about that family was that they would talk to us children like we were adults. They would listen intently to whatever we had to say, engage with us and, unlike some other neighbours, never talk over us. So, the fact that I was just twelve years old, and cold, hungry, and exhausted did not save me from her tongue. She looked at me angrily and said, "Did I not tell you to keep him out of the pub!"

When I got back home, I found out that my mother had also been praying for our safe return. Somehow, one of the neighbours had heard that Eddie was seen in Fox's earlier in the day and she had figured out what happened. She told me she would give Eddie an earful when she saw him next, but the following day I overheard her telling a neighbour about it and they were both laughing heartily.

It took me a while to see the funny side of that I can tell you. I dreamed of that Rodden's fry and the lost ten shillings for a long time!

Sally never did go back to the mart. Maggie was superstitious and said that it was God's will that she came home, and there she would stay.

I scoffed at that but stayed quiet. I did not want to risk falling out with God with my school exams coming up but could not help wondering to myself that I could have done with a bit more of His help on the long road home!

9 781527 276949